Ready... Set... GOLF!

An Essential Guide for Young Golfers

by Ann Kelly

Canadian Cataloguing in Publication Data

Kelly, Ann
Ready... Set... GOLF! An Essential Guide for Young Golfers
ISBN 978-0-9686289-1-1

1. Golf for young golfers. I. Title.

PRINTED IN CANADA

Cover art and illustration: Henrich Creative

Ready... Set... GOLF!

1. Ready... Thinking about golfing? Here are things you should know.

2. Set... Excited? Here are your next steps!

Continued on next page

3. GOLF! Time for action on the course!

Young Golfers Code

How to Use your Book!

Don't try to read it all at once.

Check the headings.

Thumb back and forth.

Jot down notes from lessons.

Mark specific sections.

Cut out the **Young Golfers Code** (page 87) and tack it on your wall!

Use the **Tracking My Progress** (page 74) and **Notes** (page 78) sections to chart your progress!

Ready... Set... GOLF!

Lucky you!

Welcome to the wonderful game of golf! Learning to play golf is not only fun but it will change your life! You will make new friends, and learn new skills! Anyone can learn to play golf and what you learn on the golf course will be of value to you in whatever you choose to do in your later life .

Do you have some of the following questions?

- *Can I play with my friends?*

- *Can I wear my runners?*

- *Do I have to take lessons?*

- *Where can I get clubs?*

- *What does 'par' mean?*

- *Can I take my iPod to the golf course?*

Answers to your questions are here! **Ready... Set... GOLF!** is for new junior golfers[1]. It tells you about the game of golf, a golf course, how to get started, the importance of lessons, the essential etiquette of golf, and countless other necessary items.

---

[1] *'Junior' Golfers are girls and boys up to the age of 17 or 18. Depending on the location, you may see other categories such as Kid's Golf, Mini-Juniors, and Junior-Juniors. This could depend on your age or your ability.*

1. ReaDy!

The Game

Your objective is to hit a golf ball from the starting area—the Tee Box—along the Fairway, and into the (4 $1/4$″ ~ 11 cm) hole on the Green. Golfers pride themselves on their honesty and always count each hit (or miss) of the ball.

A regulation game of golf consists of 18 holes.

Pssst! *New golfers often start by playing on Par 3, Executive, or 9 hole courses which should take approximately 2 hours.*

Each hole consists of a Tee Box, the Fairway, and the Green.

*   The **Tee Box (or teeing ground)**: a rectangular patch of grass from where everyone starts. Golf holes have different starting tees depending on your ability. You will usually start at the forward tee, the one closest to the fairway.

*   The **Fairway**: a stretch of mowed grass which is often lined by trees, bushes, patches of sand called bunkers, or scenic lakes or ponds.

- The **Green**: a very short cut patch of grass at the end of the fairway, where there is a flagstick in a hole.
- The **Rough** : the longer grass that borders the fairway and can be a challenge!

The more you practice and play, the better you will get, and the more fun you will have!

Equipment: What Do I NeeD?

Golf Clubs

You don't need new clubs, or many clubs, to start.
Pssst! *You should have clubs that 'fit' you. The **length** and the **weight** of the clubs are important. You could start with clubs that have been cut down, however it is preferable to use clubs made especially for juniors.*

Junior clubs will most likely be shorter, lighter and more flexible than adult clubs.

Check out the classified ads for used clubs and have an experienced golfer advise you. It's a good idea to replace the grips on used clubs that probably have become very slippery. Any Pro Shop or golf store can do this for between $5.00 and $10.00 per club.

If you are taking lessons, the teaching professional will tell you which clubs to bring to the lesson. If you're not sure... bring them all.

I have included the following information simply to help you understand what a full set of clubs could look like.

There are many combinations of clubs which players may have in their golf bags. Each club is designed to hit the ball a certain height and travel a certain distance.

1. Ready...

- **Putter**: a flat faced club used on the green. Do you know you will use a putter more than any other club in your bag?

- **Wedges**: Pitching, Sand, Lob—These are shorter clubs used around the green—they pop the ball into the air.

- **Irons**: #9, #8, #7, #6, #5, #4, #3, #2, #1

- **Hybrid, Utility, Rescue Clubs:** These clubs look like a 'fat iron' and are numbered accordingly to the loft or angle of the club face. They are a combo of an iron and a wood.

- **Woods:** #1 (driver), #3, #4, #5, #7, #9, #11
  These woods have fat heads and were originally made of wood, but now are made of many types of space-age materials!

PUTTER   IRON   WOOD

A typical bag of 14 clubs could include

- 1 *Putter*
- 1 *Sand Wedge (SW)*
- 1 *Pitching Wedge (PW)*
- 7 *Irons*
- 1 or 2 *Hybrids*
- 1 or 2 *Woods*

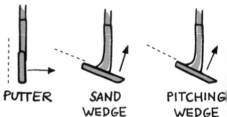

A **longer club**, like a #4 iron, will hit the ball lower and longer.

A **shorter club,** like a #9 iron, is designed to hit the ball high and a short distance.

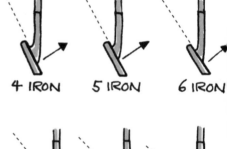

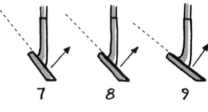

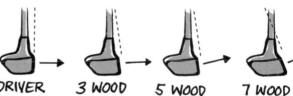

8

In the drawing at left, the dotted lines show the angle of the face of each club, and the arrows show the angle of the ball when hit with each club. As you can see, the lower the number of the club, the lower in the air the ball goes so it goes farther, and the higher the number, the higher the ball goes up, so it doesn't go as far.

The lower the number, the shorter the club; the higher the number, the longer the club.

After several practice sessions you will have a better idea what distance you will get from hitting different clubs. To help you remember, it is a good idea to create a **Cue Card,** showing the distance you hit with each of your clubs, which you could tuck in your pocket or golf bag. (*See* **Cue Card**, *page 28.*)

While casual play has no restrictions, tournament play requires that a player not carry more than 14 clubs.

Pssst! *There is no reason for a beginning junior to carry 14 clubs—they can be mighty heavy! A suggestion for a new junior would be* **putter, pitching wedge, 7 iron, 5 wood**. *You can then add other clubs to your bag as need them.*

New Golf Clubs ?

When you're ready to buy new clubs, ask a local golf professional or a golf store club fitter for their help. Most golf shops have either a hitting cage (a net) in the store or a practice range close by. You will be able to try out clubs of several different brands.

You may be able to find a 'Trade-In–Trade-Up' programs for Juniors. Check with local golf stores or Pro Shops. As you grow out of your clubs, you can trade them in and get a credit towards your next set.

Listen to the advice of the professionals.

Did you know...?

Golf club history: Up until the 1930s, clubs had names. A 3-wood was a 'spoon', a 5-iron was a 'mashie', and a 9-iron was a 'niblick'.

Golf Bag

• Most Juniors carry their clubs. A light weight golf bag with a cross shoulder strap is ideal—it helps distribute the weight evenly, and ensures better posture.

• Make sure the straps are adjusted so the bag is comfortable for YOU. The bag should rest on the lower back, just above your rear end.

• Keep the zippers closed as it is easy to drop items (balls, tees, keys, etc!) as you go along. Also, if the zippers are left gaping open, they may have a tendency to break, or the crows and squirrels may steal your goodies!

Balls

- Shiny, new balls are nice but not necessary! Good used balls are available in Pro Shops... and from relatives and friends.

- Avoid balls that look as if they've been hit too many times, are cut or badly marked, or appear stained from sitting in a creek for too long.

  I figure that these water-logged balls may just want to go right back to where they came from!

- Use a marker pen to put an identifying mark on your ball. Be creative—make up your own design!

DiD you know...?

Golf ball history: Stones, wood, feathers in a leather pouch, a rubber substance (gutta percha), then the dimpled golf ball in 1905! Today's typical golf ball has 336 dimples. Dimples reduce 'drag' so the ball goes faster, and increase 'lift' so it goes higher.

- Balls are numbered for identification—often from 1 to 8. Tell your playing partners the make and the number of your ball, ie: 'Titleist 2' or 'Callaway 4' (it is a 2 stroke penalty to hit another player's ball).

Pssst! *Of course, you can also find balls on the golf course. Make sure they're not part of someone else's game before you pick them up.*

Towel

Golf towels are used to clean the dirt and sand off clubs, or wipe your hands. On the green, when you are able to pick up your ball after having marked it, you should clean the ball so it will roll properly.

Pssst! *A face cloth does the job and is easier to carry.*

Umbrella

Golf umbrellas are generally large and do a good job of keeping you dry if it starts to pour. It's suggested that you choose one that is rain- and wind-proof.

Essential accessories in your bag

- ☐ Tees,
- ☐ balls (6–10),
- ☐ markers,
- ☐ repair tool,
- ☐ pencil,
- ☐ sun screen,
- ☐ bug spray,
- ☐ bandaid,
- ☐ $2–$5,
- ☐ water bottle,
- ☐ comb,
- ☐ energy source (nutritional snack—power bar).

Golf Clothes: What Do I wear?

(You may have everything you need in your closet!)

Golf Clothes

Dress codes at most clubs are strictly followed by everyone. This is to maintain a sense of good behavior on the golf course.

Dress like a golfer! After all, if you have set aside 4 or 5 hours to play golf it would be tough to arrive only to discover that you are not dressed properly and can't play. Don't put yourself in this embarrassing position!

There are lots of choice in styles, fabrics and colours!

Think of a collared shirt as part of your 'golf uniform'!

Look for comfort—4 hours of walking, bending and stretching!

If you look good, you will feel good... and if you feel good, you will play WELL!

Girls: Tops – shirts

- Should be easy fitting with a collar and/or sleeves.
- Logos, if any, should be small and discreet. No rock stars, commercials, political statements, or the like!

Bottoms – pants

- Long pants, Capri pants, shorts, skorts and skirts.
- Length of shorts, skorts and skirts = just above the knee.
- Look for deep accessible pockets.
- No sweat pants, no jeans.

Boys: Tops – shirts

- Collar and sleeves.

- Shirt tails tucked in.

- Despite soaring temperatures—tops must be worn at all times on the course.

- Logos, if any, should be small and discreet.
  No rock stars, commercials, political statements, or the like!

Bottoms – pants

- Slacks, long shorts.

- Look for deep, easily-accessible pockets on both sides.

- No torn or ragged cut-offs. No sweat pants. No jeans.

Footwear

Golf shoes are usually lace-up shoes, which have soft spikes on the soles to keep you from slipping when you swing the club. They also improve performance by supporting better balance. Keep your shoes clean!

Pssst! *Although you may start to play in sturdy runners, golf shoes are mandatory at many clubs.*

Socks

Ankle to knee length—usually depends on the weather.
Pssst! *Believe it or not, many private clubs require a specific sock length!*

Rain / Cold weather gear

Be ready with a light sweater and/or water resistant jacket in your bag… you could start playing in brilliant sunshine and suddenly be pelted with rain. A jacket should 'breathe', be a soft quiet fabric, and allow you to swing freely.

Glove

While not required, a golf glove helps in gripping the club. If you are right-handed the glove goes on the left hand, and vice-versa for lefties. Gloves should fit snugly.

Hat/Visor

A hat or visor is important on the golf course. The brim offers good protection from the sun (or rain), and can help cut down the distraction of movement around you (your buddies chatting or fiddling with their clubs) and give you better focus on the ball.

The brim of the hat or visor should always face forward.

Take your hat off before entering the clubhouse!

Did you know...?

Golfers shout 'Fore' when they hit a shot that goes astray, to alert other players to watch out for the ball. 'Fore' is an old Scottish warning meaning, 'Look out ahead!'.

Bonus, Bonus, Bonus!

So, you are going to have fun; learn a new game and make new friends! As a bonus you will also be learning the following values which will last you for a lifetime!

- **Honesty** Doing what is right even when no one is watching. Count all your strokes!

- **Sportsmanship** Being a graceful winner and loser. Know and play within the rules!

- **Respect** Being respectful to yourself, your partners, your opponents and the golf course.

- **Confidence** Learning to trust and have confidence in your abilities.

- **Responsibility** Being accountable for your actions on the golf course actions. Leave the course in better condition than you found it.

- **Perseverance** Learning to persist despite obstacles. Quickly forget a poor stroke or a bad bounce and move on.

- **Integrity** Setting and maintaining a high standard for personal conduct on the course.

- **Courtesy** Being considerate and thoughtful toward others. Silent and still as others are hitting.

- **Judgement** Being able to weigh all factors before taking action.

- **Managing emotions** Being able to perform in stressful situations

- **Social skills** Learning to relate to people of all ages, backgrounds and interests.

Did you know...?

The oldest continually operating golf club in North America is the Royal Montreal, in Quebec, Canada, formed in 1873

2. SET!

Lessons: Do I need them?

Yes! Lessons from a qualified professional are fun and important!

While you can learn a lot about this game yourself through golf magazines and videos, it is recommended that you take lessons.

You will learn how to stand, how to grip the club, ball position and the many parts to a good swing that will enable you to hit the little ball! This could take some time, so please be patient!

Pssst! Although it may be helpful at first, DO NOT rely on friends or relatives to help you get better at this game.

21

Where will I go for lessons?

Lessons for Juniors are usually after school, weekends and holidays. Check out local Junior Clinics and Junior Camps— these are often a great deal and a great way to meet new golfing friends! As well there are programs in some schools.

- **Group lessons** are often given at golf courses, driving ranges, the local community college or through recreation programs. Ask for recommendations from friends or relatives who golf.

- **Private lessons** at a golf course or driving range usually last 1/2 hour and cost from $15–$30. They often come in 3- or 4-lesson packages.

- After a lesson, try to spend several sessions practising what you learned! You will be surprised at how quickly you can improve!

Pssst! *What about asking for a set of lessons as a gift... such as a birthday present!*

DiD you know...?

The Longest Hole in the World is at the Satsuki Golf Club in Sano, Japan. The 7th hole (par 7) measures 964 yards!

What is expected from you as a golf student

- Know where you are to meet your instructor

- Be on time, or preferably 10–15 minutes early to warm up

- Be dressed appropriately with the correct equipment

- Be enthusiastic and ready to learn.

- You may want to write notes—bring a small note pad, or this book

What should be expected from your teaching professional

- Lessons starting on time

- Clear simple instructions

- Activity

- Some individual attention

- Practice drills

- Fun!

Learning from one professional as opposed to many different instructors is preferred… as long as you are making progress and are enjoying the lessons.

Practice: This Will Pay Off!

It is a known fact that 60–70% of your score will come from your Short Game—these are shots from close to the green and on the green. Time spent practising putting, chipping and pitching will pay-off 'big-time' on the golf course and lower your score quickly.

The Practice Putting Green

- This area is usually near a golf clubhouse and/or the first tee. Only use your putter. If there are others practising on the putting green use a maximum of 3 balls. Practice with a purpose—give yourself some challenges.

- There are also putting areas at many Practice ranges.

Pssst! *You do not need a special facility to practice putting—how about putting on a carpet in your house? A tipped cup or a table leg would be a fine target.*

The Practice Chipping/Pitching/ Bunker Area

- Learn these specialized short shots. They are very useful around the green and can lower your score!

- Be very careful and do not hit in the direction of another person.

Pssst! *You do not need a specialized facility... what about your back yard, a small patch of grass in a park, or a vacant lot... and using a laundry basket or box for a target?*

The Chip: A putt with a pump start, little air and more roll

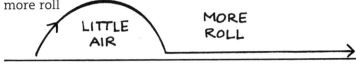

The Pitch: Pitch is like a rainbow—more air, little roll

25

The Practice Range (often called the Driving Range)

The term 'driving range' is a misnomer, because golfers use the range for practising with all clubs in their bag, not just their drivers!

- Look neat—wear your golf clothes and golf shoes!

- Pay for a bucket of practice balls at the counter. You may be given a token to use at a ball machine where you will get your bucket of balls. (Place your bucket correctly in the machine before inserting your token or a small avalanche of balls will very quickly litter the ground at your feet!)

- Always give other golfers lots of room when passing behind them on the range! A club can really hurt!

- Find an empty stall, set your equipment down, stretch, take several easy warm-up swings with your shorter club before starting to hit balls.

Pssst! *Although it is VERY tempting... never attempt to retrieve golf balls on the range.*

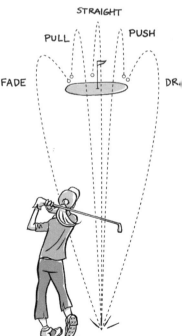

26

Suggested practice routines—
Challenge yourself! Practice with a Purpose!

- **Practice** what you have just learned in a lesson.

- **Start using your smaller, shorter clubs** then move to your longer clubs. Finally when you are nicely warmed up you will be ready to use your driver.

- **Change your target** with each shot.

- **Play virtual golf**. Imagine a golf hole... then play it! Hit with your driver, figure out where you landed and how far to the next imaginary spot, then use the appropriate club to hit the next shot. You will use many different clubs from your bag—just like on the course.

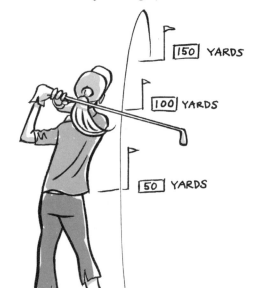

150 YARDS

100 YARDS

50 YARDS

Your cue carD

The Practice Range is an ideal place to create your own Cue Card which will help you remember the approximate distances that you can hit the ball with your different clubs. Tuck this into a pocket or your golf bag to use as a reminder.

Pssst! *Remember to spend time on the putting and chipping areas—this is where you can really cut strokes off your score!*

Where Can I Play?

You may be lucky enough to live near a golf course, or have a relative or friend who plays at a certain course. **Junior memberships** are a super bargain at most courses. Often lessons are available and the fees are minimal.

Golf courses love to have a good number of junior golfers— they know that once you get hooked on the game you will be a golfer for many years!

Club members you may not know are often willing to **sponsor** new junior golfers. If you need a sponsor to join a certain club, check with the Pro Shop.

Juniors may have their own locker room in a club house. You may only be able to play at specific times. And, due to liquor laws in different locations, you may be restricted as to where you are allowed in a clubhouse.

Golf courses generally fall into the following types.

- **Public Courses**: Any golfer may phone and arrange tee times. (*See **Tee Times**, page 31.*)

- **Par 3 Courses**: usually public with only short par 3 holes—excellent for practising your short game! Highly recommended for new juniors.

- **Executive Courses**: These courses are shorter in length than a regulation 18 hole course. They can be either 9 or 18 holes. Nine holes are recommended for new juniors.

- **Regulation 18 Hole Course**: These courses are not recommended for new golfers. Once a player has reached a certain familiarity with golf skills, rules and etiquette, these courses will then provide 4 hours of challenge and fun.

- **Semi-private Courses**: Golfers may buy a membership which gives them the privileges of private courses and often a lower green fee than non-members. Non-members may phone and book tee times as well.

- **Private Courses**: Generally an initial joining fee and a yearly membership fee are required, which give privileges of a locker, club storage, club cleaning, shoe cleaning, and no green fees. Non-members would be allowed as guests of a member and a green fee will be charged.

- **Mini Golf**: Don't forget mini-golf! Improve your putting! Fun for all your friends!

Tee times

Many clubs have specific times for Juniors to play. The pro shop staff will assist you in reserving a time

An alternative is to be a 'walk-on' during Junior play time. This means you show up at the course and ask if there is a tee-time available for you.

Pssst! *Tee times are 7/8/9 minutes apart and that's why you will be given some seemingly strange times like 8:24 or 9:59.*

Arrive at the course about **30 minutes ahead** of your tee time and come dressed to play. This allows you to check in to the pro shop, pay your green fee, put your shoes on, practice putting or warm up by hitting some balls on the practice range.

2. set...

Did you know...?

The PGA has a long standing policy of not letting players wear shorts in tournament play.

Around the Clubhouse

- **The Pro Shop:** This is where you check in on arrival— look for the signs! It is a small store that specializes in golf clothing, golf accessories and golf clubs. Tee times and golf lessons are also booked through the Pro Shop.

- **Food:** There may be a small restaurant in the clubhouse, a snack shack between the ninth and tenth hole, (here you must 'grab and run' unless you want to lose your place to the foursome following you.)

- **Warm-Up / Practice Facilities:** These could be a driving/practice range, a putting green, a chipping/ pitching area and a practice bunker area.

- **Washrooms:** usually found in the clubhouse locker room, at the ninth hole, and discreetly located elsewhere on the course. It may help to know where they are located before starting a round of golf!

  Pssst! *It's a good idea to use the washroom before heading out to practice or play!*

Useful tidbits

- **Can my friends walk with me as I play?** Most courses strongly discourage or disallow non-golfers walking on the course for safety reasons. Only playing golfers are allowed on most courses, and each golfer must have their own golf clubs.

- **Thunderstorms can be deadly on a golf course.** If a storm with lightning is approaching, don't think you'll 'just finish playing the hole'. Leave the course immediately!

- **Cell phones:** Turn off your cell phone and tuck it into your bag.

- **iPods:** These are discouraged at golf courses—an exception might be practice areas.

2. set...

Did you know...?

There are 18 holes on a golf course because that's how many there were at St. Andrews in Scotland in the 1890s, when its rules were adopted by golf clubs in the UK.

To Carry, to Pull or to Ride?

- **Walking**: Most juniors walk and carry their clubs—a light weight bag is preferable. Bags must be kept off the Tee Box, the Green, and the fringe around the Green.

- **Pull carts:** These can be rented (sometimes free!) at most courses. Make sure that the bag is well anchored on the Pull Cart. It is easy to tip the whole cart when climbing a hill, or catch a wheel when crossing a bridge, and it is time-consuming (and messy) to gather everything up.

  Make sure the cart is stable, and will not roll and hit something, or head into the lake, before leaving it to putt.

- **Riding—power carts**: A person must have a valid driver's license to drive a power cart. They are powerful machines and may look harmless, but if not operated properly they can be very dangerous.

Pssst! *Never put your golf bag, your pull cart or the power cart on the Tee Box or the Green.* The course superintendent has worked very hard to groom these areas. Please don't damage them.

Playing a Golf Course

A regulation game of golf is 18 holes.

Each regulation golf course will have a combination of shorter Par 3, Par 4 and longer Par 5 holes. This indicates the number of strokes expert golfers should take to play the hole.

The Par on a hole includes 2 strokes on the green.

For example,

- A Par 3 hole is a hole on which a player would take one stroke from the tee box to the green, then 2 strokes on the green to get the ball into the hole.

- A Par 5 means three strokes to get to the green plus 2 strokes for putting into the hole.

PAR 3

PAR 4

PAR 5

35

The par for an 18 hole course is a combination of strokes on all the holes and is generally around 72.

The new golfer should not be concerned with a course's par rating, but simply try to play each hole in as few strokes as possible. And always play from the forward tees.

Types of golf holes you may come across...

2. Set...

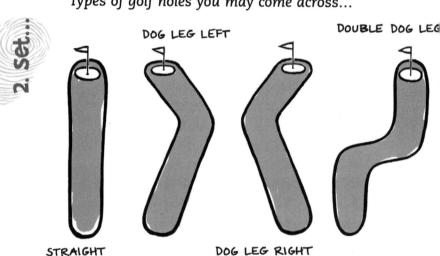

DOG LEG LEFT

DOUBLE DOG LEG

STRAIGHT
AWAY

DOG LEG RIGHT

Who will want to golf with me?

Who are you?

Respectful, happy, fun, cheerful, thoughtful, kind, pleasant? Or

Moody, sulky, crabby, temperamental, testy, gloomy, angry?

Who would you like to play golf with?

Golfers of any age or skill level will enjoy playing with you. What is important to other players is...

- your ability to keep up a good pace,

- your knowledge of the rules and etiquette, and

- your awareness of what others in your group are doing on the course.

2. Set...

WHO WOULD YOU LIKE TO PLAY GOLF WITH ?

Whenever possible play with someone who is better than you. Watch what they do and how they react to good and poor shots.

- **Compliment** good shots.

- **Be encouraging and positive** but avoid offering advice to others unless asked.

- Golfers are concerned about their own shots and not interested in hearing what may have gone wrong with your shot. Hit a poor shot? Why? **Learn from it!** Grumble to yourself for 5 seconds then move on.

- Remember that everyone on the course has set aside time and money to have fun and enjoy a game of golf. **Be thoughtful of others** by keeping up a good pace and keeping noise to a minimum. Golf is a quiet game!

DiD you know...?

'Birdie' (one under par) comes from 19th Century American slang, meaning something particularly great.

3. GOLF!... Action!!

The Tee Box—
Teeing Off

Getting ready to hit on the tee box can sometimes make
you nervous, but helping you feel more comfortable is what
this book is all about. Also check out The Mental Game.
(*See* What's going on between your ears?, *page 62.*)

Be Prepared! Arrive early!

- A suggestion: In one pocket you need 1 ball,
  2 ball markers, 2 tees and a repair tool.
  In the other pocket you could carry
  another ball—just in case your first ball
  lands in trouble (oops!)—you won't
  waste time going to your bag
  to dig out another ball.

- Introduce yourself to
  the other players in
  your group. Everyone
  can identify the ball
  they are playing with.

1 BALL
2 MARKERS
2 TEES →
1 REPAIR TOOL

3. GOLF!

39

- Never swing the club in the direction of another player—a small rock or piece of grass could easily fly into someone's face.

- Tee Boxes often have 4 or 5 sets of different colored markers between which the ball is placed. Beginning golfers usually use the **forward tees**.

- **'Ready golf'** is a term often used on the tee box—it simply means the person who is ready can step up and hit their ball. It is a way to speed up play.

3. GOLF!

DiD you know...?

It's not known exactly where the word 'caddy' comes from, but it might be from 'cadet', as army cadets carried the golf clubs for royalty in France.

Teeing Off

- Start once the group ahead of you is clearly out of your driving distance.

- Stand off to the side, at least 8–10 feet from a player who is getting ready to hit. Be silent and still. Whispering is disconcerting and even scratching your nose can be distracting.

- When it's your turn, place your ball on a tee between, or behind (up to 2 club lengths), the tee-markers. The tee box is the only place you can use a tee.

- Your first drive may be a nerve-racking one—that 'everyone is watching me feeling'. It may be helpful to use your favorite club.

- One practice swing is considered sufficient and will do minimal damage to the tee box. Swing smoothly!

- Watch to see where your ball lands! If you cannot see it land, choose a tree or bush in the direction the ball was heading and, once all players have hit, head in that direction. Also, watch where your partners' balls land— this will help speed up play.

Hurrah! the game has begun! Everyone goes directly to their ball while planning to hit their next shot.

3. GOLF!

The Fairway

Yippee! your ball is probably on or near the fairway. If not, you'll have the challenge of dealing with the hazards! *(See Hazards, page 28.)*

- **Estimate** the distance from your ball to the flagstick. The 150-yard (or metre) markers are often on both sides of the fairway. These could be stakes, rocks, bushes, or special trees. The 150 yard marker could also be a post or a disc on the fairway. Other yardages are often marked on the fairway by tags on the sprinkler heads. These distances are usually marked to the center of the green. Know which club you will need for the desired distance. *(Refer to your Cue Card—page 28.)*

- **Bring your clubs close to your ball**; off to the side and out of the way of your swing. This saves time as you will not have to walk back to pick them up. This is called 'good course management'!

- **Be ready** to play when it's your turn.

- Do not pick up or otherwise touch your ball until you reach the green. **Pssst!** *If you are a beginner in a fun game, most players will not object if you move it with your club out of a difficult situation.*

- **Stand off to the side** of a player who is hitting their ball. Be SILENT and STILL.

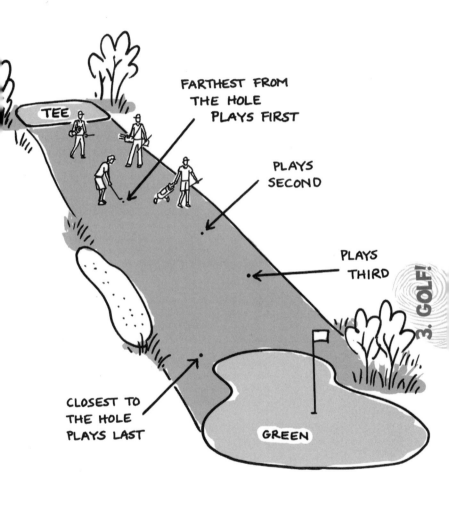

FARTHEST FROM
THE HOLE
PLAYS FIRST

PLAYS
SECOND

PLAYS
THIRD

TEE

CLOSEST TO
THE HOLE
PLAYS LAST

GREEN

3. GOLF!

- **Yell 'fore'** as quickly and loudly as possible if your ball is headed towards another player! (An apology to that player at an opportune time is important.) If, on the other hand, you hear someone holler that same word... quickly cover your head, duck and pray. This is the ONLY time that yelling is acceptable on a golf course! Exception: Golfers can appreciate cheering for a Hole In One!

- The player who is furthest from the green will hit first and then the others will follow.

- **Repair a divot** if you sent a small patch of grass flying when you made your shot? Retrieve and replace the grass and tamp it down with your foot. Alternatively, sand bottles may be provided to fill the hole.

- **Maintain a steady pace**—play each hole without delay. VERY IMPORTANT!

- **When hitting to the green**, wait until the group ahead is well off the green

All golfers have days/holes when they struggle and their swing does not seem to be working. This can become tiring and discouraging.

As a new golfer... just pick your ball up after 4–6 hits, take it to the green and putt with the others.

All golfers make mistakes... it's how you recover from these errors that counts! Same as in everyday life!

Remember, it's only a game, it will get better, so settle yourself down and get ready for the next hole.

Did you know...?

In 1985, a golfer at the Bangkok Country Club in Thailand hit his tee shot off the 17th into the water... but it ended up on the bank! The ball had hit and bounced off the back of a large fish!

Could be Trouble! ~ Lost Balls

Trees, bushes and long grass...

Lost a ball? Look quickly: if you can't find it within two minutes (although the rules allow you 5), drop another ball from your bag and add two strokes to your score. Eventually you must learn the rules of golf that apply to these situations.

3. GOLF!

DiD you know...?

In 1906, Goodrich introduced a golf ball with a rubber core filled with compressed air, called the Pneumatic. The ball was outlawed because it tended to explode mid-air, or even worse, in a golfer's pocket.

Could be More Trouble! ~ Hazards

Water

- Experienced players do not worry about the water holes on the course, but it can be scary for the beginner. Picture where you want the ball to end up, keep your eye on the ball, and swing smoothly. The ball will go up and over! If you look up too soon, your club will lift up, and you will likely see your ball splash in the water.

- If you have hit your ball into the water and can see it… use a retriever (a long pole with a scoop), then drop the ball and add 1 stroke. (See **Rules**, page 54.)

- If you cannot get your ball from the water, kiss it goodbye, drop another in line with the point where it entered the water. Hit away and add 1 stroke. (See **Rules**, page 54.)

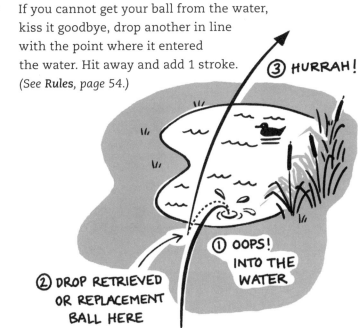

③ HURRAH!

3. GOLF!

① OOPS! INTO THE WATER

② DROP RETRIEVED OR REPLACEMENT BALL HERE

Bunker

Sand shots in the bunker can be fun—once you learn how to hit them!

- You may not touch the sand with your club ('ground your club') before you hit the ball.

- You may not clean up any debris, such as leaves or twigs in the bunker before you hit the ball.

- After you have successfully hit the ball out of the bunker, use the rake and smooth the sand for the following players.

- If you have tried to hit your ball a couple of times and are no further along—toss the ball out of the bunker, rake the sand and continue. Not allowed in a tournament!

A 'Golden Ferret': A ball out of the sand and into the hole! This expression is used often in the UK.

Rakes: In or out of the bunker? Simply put the rake back where you found it!

Did you know...?

Recovering lost golf balls legally from water hazards is a $1 million a week business involving divers and ball-scavenging vacuum systems.

Putting ~ The Green

Hurrah! The practice putting you've done will pay off!

- **Leave your clubs** between the green and the path to the next tee box. This is important as you can easily pick them up on the way to the next tee box. You will not waste time going back to the front of the green and you will not annoy following golfers who are approaching the green. Good course management!

- **Once all balls are on the green everyone should mark their ball** (the little disc marker that is in your pocket is placed, without touching the ball, directly behind the ball, then the ball is picked up). The player who is closest to the flagstick takes it out of the hole and places it softly on the ground so it is out of the way of any ball being putted.

LEAVE GOLF
BAGS HERE

NEXT TEE

GREEN

DIRECTION
OF PLAY

- **Repair** the dent your ball made on the green with your repair tool. Use a prying motion to move the grass to the center of the dent, then flatten the surface with your putter.

- **Avoid stepping** on the 'line' of others' putts. Your footprint could cause their ball to go off course.

  BE SILENT AND STILL when a player is putting

- **The person whose ball is furthest from the hole putts first**—if that ball does not go in, that player can either continue putting or can mark the ball in the new position. The next player to putt is now the farthest away from the hole—and so it goes until everyone has putted into the hole ('putted out').

- **To replace a ball that has been marked,** reverse the procedure: place the ball directly in front of the marker then pick up the marker.

- **To speed up play,** a putt very close to the hole may be called a 'gimme' or players may say 'it's yours'; then you can pick the ball up and count the pick-up as one stroke. Not allowed in a tournament!

- **Tending the flagstick:** If a player can't see the hole because of distance from the hole or bumps in the green, another person may be asked to 'tend' the flagstick. That person stands out to the side of the hole, with one hand on the flagstick, ready to pull it out. **Pssst!** *It is a penalty against the putter if the ball hits the flagstick.* The person tending the flagstick should make sure his/her shadow does not cover the hole.

- Once your ball is in the hole, retrieve it!

- **Check** that no clubs are left behind as you leave the green.

- **Move** to the next tee box, **THEN** record your score.

Thanking your Playing Partners

At the end of the game leave the green quickly. **Shake hands** (hats off for boys) with all members of your group (yes, all your buddies!... and even your brother, sister, Mom or Dad!) and thank them for the game.

Very Important!

Pace of Play

When you first start playing on a golf course you may feel rushed. This feeling will lessen as your game improves and as you quickly catch on to the following tips.

- You should have the ability to maintain a **vigorous, steady pace.**

- **Walk smartly** on the course, or to and from your cart.

- **Continually prepare** for your next shot.

- **Arm yourself** with extra balls, tees and markers.

- **Track everyone's shots**—saves time looking for balls.

- **Take your bag** to the ball.

- **Hit when ready** as long as there is no danger to others.

- **'Hole out' or continuous putt.**

- **Line up your putt** while others are putting—without disturbing anyone.

- **Keep up** to the group ahead of you.

- After finishing a hole **go directly** to the next tee box *before* recording scores.

3. GOLF!

53

What Rules Should I Know?

There are lots of rules in this great game, but don't worry, you'll pick them up quickly and keep learning them as you play.

As a new golfer don't be shy about telling your fellow golfers that you may need help on some of the rules. **Pssst!** *To get you started... here are a couple of simplified rules:*

- Your ball must be played from behind an imaginary line between the two markers on the tee box.

- The ball must be played **as it lies**. You may not improve the ball's position, even in long grass—so trying to keep it on the fairway is a good plan!

- **Hazards: Water, Bunkers**

  1. If your ball lands in a hazard, **you may not 'ground your club'** in that hazard before striking it. This means you can take a practice swing, but the club must not touch the hazard (water, sand).

  2. If your ball lands in the water (marked by yellow stakes), **quickly retrieve it if possible**, or kiss it good-bye! and drop another ball behind the point of entry. Take one stroke penalty in either case.

  3. If your ball lands in a lateral hazard (marked by red stakes) **you may drop another ball** within two club lengths of entry and no closer to the hole. Take a one stroke penalty.

3. GOLF!

Did you know...?

The highest operating 18-hole golf club in the world is in Bolivia—La Paz Golf Club at 10,800 feet.

Ready... Set... GOLF!

- **Unplayable lies** (this is when you can't get a decent swing at the ball, such as if it lies in a clump of bushes): you have three options, each with a one stroke penalty.

  1. Declare your ball 'unplayable' and go back to the place from where you hit your last shot and hit another, or

  2. retrieve the ball and drop it within 2 club lengths, no closer to the hole, or

  3. retrieve the ball and drop it on an imaginary line from the unplayable lie through the flagstick. Go as far back as you wish.

- **Lost ball**: If you think, after striking your ball, that your ball may be lost, immediately hit another ball (a declared provisional ball) which you will use if you are unable to find the first one. If you did not hit a 'provisional,' go back to the place where you hit your last ball and hit another!

  A ball is always dropped with arm extended horizontally from the shoulder.

When you start to play in a league, a regular game or a tournament, an official rule book is essential! Eventually you are responsible for knowing the rules.

Pssst! *Attend Rules Clinics whenever you get a chance! I guarantee you will always learn something new! And the rules could make for a good trivia game with your golfing friends.*

3. GOLF!

Scoring

When you first start to play, the scoring is often confusing and you may lose track of your shots. There are several possible solutions:

1. Don't count.
2. Count only excellent shots.
3. Count only the 'good' holes.

As you improve, the number of shots you take on each hole will decrease and keeping track will be easier.

Golf is a Game of Honour

Once you have decided to keep your score, it is imperative to be honest in recording your scores and to remember that you are playing against yourself. If you lose track or are confused about your score on a hole ask another player to quickly help you re-count it. If you lie about your score your scores, you are only fooling yourself and you don't want the reputation of being a cheat!

Did you know...?

Gene Sarazen created the first sand wedge in 1933.

3. GOLF!

Scoring Terms

Par	=	The number of strokes an expert golfer should have on each hole. This is shown on the score card.
Par minus 1 stroke	=	Birdie
Par minus 2 strokes	=	Eagle
Par minus 3 strokes	=	Albatross—A very rare bird!—Truly amazing!
PAR + 1 stroke	=	Bogey *(not bad!)*
PAR + 2 strokes	=	Double Bogey *(ugh)*
PAR + 3 strokes	=	Triple Bogey *(ugh ugh)*
Hole-in-One	=	A Miracle! Someday you'll get one!

Handicap

Handicap is a term you will hear often. It is an indicator of the skill level of the golfer. The lower the handicap, the better the player.

A person's handicap is established after 5–10 game scores have been recorded. All the calculations are done by a computer—phew!

For a beginning golfer, a good focus is to **play against the golf course**. Try to better your score each time you play. Using the same score card for several games is an interesting way to track your progress.

As you improve you can have fun playing against others. This is where the handicap system will make it a fair competition.

DiD you know...?

The first lady to play golf in Scotland was Mary, Queen of Scots, in the 1500s. She was later beheaded; this was not related to her golf game.

Understanding the Score Card

1 Number of the hole

2 Yardage

3 PAR for the hole

4 HDCP: Each hole is 'handicapped' as to its difficulty. For example, on this card, Men's hole #3 and Ladies' hole #5 is the most difficult on which to get par, and Men's hole #15 and Ladies' hole #15 are much easier.

5 Area to record names. Scores will be recorded under players' names.

6 PAR for the course

7 Ratings which are important when it comes to comparing scores on different courses

8 Net score: the result of your score minus your handicap. (See **Handicap**, page 59.)

Pssst! On the reverse side of a score card, there are often local rules for that specific course. Remember to read them—it may save you some strokes!

3. GOLF!

60

Player _____ **7** _____ Date _____

RATINGS	RED	WHITE	BLUE												
Men	68.1	69.6	71.0	Men		Andy	Sue	Pat	Alice **5**					Women	
Women	74.5	76.7	--												

	RED	WHITE	BLUE	PAR	HDCP									PAR	HDCP
1 1	367	382	397	4	11									4	7
2	364	374	408	4	9									4	11
3	389	396	420	4	1									5	3
4	150	154	155	3	13									3	15
5	486	506	515	5	5									5	1
6	396	403	429	4	3									5	9
7	126	149	160	3	17									3	17
8	322	322	327	4	15									4	13
9	366	385	405	4	7									4	5
OUT	2966	3071	3216	35										37	

10	404	415	430	4	4									5	14
11	163	209	237	3	14									3	16
12	409	416	423	4	2									5	6
13	334	346	386	4	12									4	4
14	418	463	494	5	10									5	2
15	145	157	157	3	18									3	18
16	369	379	385	4	8									4	8
17	365	382	400	4	16									4	12
18	341	396	414	4	6									4	10
IN	2948	3163	3326	35										37	
OUT	2966	3071	3216	35										37	
TOTAL	5912	6234	6542	70										74	
SIGNED: SCORER				**7**		HDCP		**8**					SIGNED: PLAYER		
						NET									

SLOPE RATING   MEN   RED: 124   WHITE:127   BLUE: 130
                WOMEN   RED: 135   WHITE: 140

3. GOLF!

What is going on 'Between your ears'?

If you think you can, or if you think you can't, you're right!

The mental game

Your ball has just landed in the sand! And you say or think 'Oh, I hate the sand!' This may guarantee that you will be in the sand longer than you ever imagined.

Your ball is on the green 25 feet from the hole. You say or think, 'I'll never make it from here'. And you won't!

Your 'self-talk' or 'self-think' is very important in the game of golf. These are the thoughts that you say to yourself on a continuous basis. It is important to be positive about the challenges you face on the golf course.

Some positive self-talk would be

I can hit this ball.

I can hit it out of the rough.

I am good at getting out of the sand.

I am a good putter.

I can do this!

A combination of golf lessons, practice sessions, and positive self-talk will give you a 1 – 2 – 3 punch!

Pssst! *Focus where you want the ball to land, imagine the flight of the ball to that point, and swing.*

Another tip Never give up on a golf course! Your next shot is a 'new' shot. The next hole is a 'new' hole. The next nine is a 'new' nine. You may start out poorly, but persevere and you could end up having the best game of your life.

The title of this book can help you focus:

Ready... Set... GOLF!

1. **Ready...** this is when you think and make decisions (what club, what target)

2. **Set...** this is when you set up (stance, posture, grip)

3. **GOLF!** Stop thinking! It is action time—trust yourself and swing away!

Marshals
(or Ranger/Player Assistant)

Hey!—the Marshal is your friend!!

Many courses have a Marshal. His/her duty is to help everyone on the course enjoy the game by keeping play moving.

At any one time there could be over 140 other golfers on a course. Most clubs expect golfers to finish 18 holes of golf in 4–4.25 hours.

Stay close to the group in front of you. If you lose sight of the group ahead, alert your fellow players and speed up your game.

If slow, the Marshal may ask your group to let the following group 'play through'. This means that you stand aside and let the following group play ahead. Good golf etiquette means letting that group play through even without the Marshal's request.

The Marshal also can help finding 'left-behind' clubs or headcovers.

Grounds Crew

Each morning before you get out of bed, there is a 'silent army' of grounds workers busy preparing the golf course for you.

All golf courses have a Grounds Superintendent who is responsible for the condition on the course.

- They are knowledgeable people who have countless certificates and diplomas received after studying many areas about golf courses and the environment.

- They supervise a crew who mow, repair, water, and keep the course in excellent shape.

Be respectable of their work, thank them or wave when you see them.

Leave all parts of the course better than you found it!

Did you know that an unrepaired ball mark on the green takes 2–3 weeks to heal. **Repair your ball marks** and any others that you see, then they will heal in half the time.

3. GOLF!

Did you know...?

There are 3 golf balls on the moon.

competition!

Congratulations! You know the etiquette, your skills are improving, you know most of the rules, you have the time... and you've decided to enter a tournament!

Be sure you are entering into competition for the correct reasons... to test your skills in the competitive environment and see where you stand with your fellow competitors. It's fun to compete against others, especially when you do well.

Pssst! *Golf is really a game between you and the course, and you always win when you do your best!*

3. GOLF!

As a competitive golfer you must be prepared to...

- look after your own equipment—mark your ball, count your clubs (only 14 allowed),

- know the rules,

- finish the game you start; never leave the course unless injured or told to get off the course,

- complete the round unless injured or play is suspended,

- compete in any weather,

- enjoy your playing partners and the friendships you make through golf.

Let the competition begin!

- You will probably be nervous, but remember others are nervous too!

- When you feel tense during competition...
  1. check your fundamentals (grip, stance, etc), and
  2. use the shots you are comfortable with.

- Ask for a Rules Official to answer to any situations about which you are puzzled, or play a second ball and inform the official at the end of your round.

- It is the responsibility of each player to keep score for each hole, check for accuracy and sign the score card when finished.

Be Mindful!

- Many things, over which you have no control, affect a game of golf. Examples would be; the weather (wind, sun, rain, temperature), your playing partners, the course condition, and the pace of other golfers.

  Luckily, there are many things you can control.... You can control your behavior—how you react to difficult situations, your equipment, your preparation, your pace of play, and your attitude. Always do your best on each shot and try to learn from your mistakes before your next competition.

  Learn to accept those things that you cannot control— prepare for those you can control!

- The best place for spectators is off to the side of the play.

- Interference by parents or friends can result in penalties against you!

A Final Note: Never give up and always do your best!

Pssst! *Lots of behind-the-scenes work has gone into a tournament—always remember to thank volunteers, officials and staff.*

Types of Tournaments

Medal play/Stroke play: the player having the lowest score wins. (Gross winner = total strokes. Net winner = score minus handicap)

Match play: two golfers play against each other. The golfer winning the most holes is the winner.

Scramble: a common team format. Everyone on a four/five person team takes their shot, walks up the fairway together and decides which one of the four shots is the best. The others then pick up their balls and play the next shot from that spot.

Stableford: a method of scoring that uses a point system and a player's handicap.
4 points – eagle
3 points – birdie
2 points – par
1 point – bogey

Best Ball: usually played by 2 player teams – the lowest individual's score score on a hole counts as the team score for the hole.

Shotgun: Every player/team starts playing at the same time on different holes of the course. Tournaments often use a 'shot gun' start. Everyone finishes at the same time which is convenient for a shared meal and prize giving.

Resources

Junior Clinics/Leagues

- Most locations (Counties, States, Provinces, areas/ zones) have extensive Junior Programs. Google 'junior golf' in your area to see what is available.

- Attend all the Clinics you can—you will continue to learn at each one!

- Once you have mastered some of the skills of this game and know the rules and etiquette, take a chance—join a league!

You will have the opportunity of meeting new players, playing with players of similar ability and perhaps participating in skill and rules clinics scheduled especially for your group.

3. GOLF!

Plus...

The Golf Channel – Good for picking up helpful hints

Golf Tournaments on TV – More exposure to the game

Volunteering – Assist in a Golf Tournaments in your area

Monthly Golf Magazines – Excellent articles.

PGA Junior program – www.thefirsttee.org

The Internet – this could keep you busy for hours!

A Mentor – A friend or acquaintance who you could ask for help

Books, Video Tapes – Lots of these available in bookstores, golf stores or your local library.

Golf Rules – Quick Reference by Yves TonThat = excellent rule book

Did you know...?

Several countries require players to have passed a theory exam and proven competent playing ability before being allowed to play on certain golf courses.

Hints from other Junior golfers!

- Be honest, always count all your strokes!

- Remember that sometimes golf can be frustrating— being patient will pay off.

- Be polite.

- While tending the flagstick, grab the flag to stop it from flapping.

- Enter a bunker from the flattest area close to your ball (and rake as you leave!).

- Always be prepared with lots of balls in your bag.

- If you want to take a drink or change a jacket, do it after you hit the ball.

3. GOLF!

Please add to this list!

Any suggestions from Junior golfers will be appreciated! Contact me, ann.kelly@shaw.ca with YOUR favourite Hints and I will include them in a next printing.

My hints:

. . . .

. . . .

. . . .

. . . .

. . . .

. . . .

. . . .

. . . .

. . . .

. . . .

. . . .

3. GOLF!

Use the following chart to help you see how you are improving and what you need to practice.

3. GOLF!

Tracking my Progress!

DATE	LOCATION	SCORE / NUMBER OF PUTTS

HAPPY WITH...	NEEDS WORK ON...

3. GOLF!

🏌 Ready... Set... GOLF!

Tracking my Progress!

DATE	LOCATION	SCORE / NUMBER OF PUTTS

HAPPY WITH...	NEEDS WORK ON...

3. GOLF!

Notes (or... what I learned today!)

. . . .

. . . .

. . . .

. . . .

. . . .

. . . .

. . . .

. . . .

. . . .

3. GOLF!

. . . .

. . . .

. . . .

. . . .

. . . .

. . . .

. . . .

. . . .

. . . .

3. GOLF!

Golf talk!

'You have the honor'

> The person who scores the lowest on a given hole earns the right to tee up first on the next hole.

'Drive for show, putt for dough'

> A reminder that putting can be more important than driving.

'Take a Mulligan'

> This is a second attempt on a first shot—usually on the first hole. It is illegal but often used in a friendly social game.

'A gimme is not a gift'

> This is a short putt that you are not asked to hit because it is assumed that you would make it. Although it is called a gimme and you have not hit the ball, you must add the stroke to your score.

'Swing easy in the breezy'

> A reminder that you don't have to swing harder in windy conditions.

'Never short on a birdie putt'

> A reminder that your ball will never go in the hole if it is short.

3. GOLF!

'This game is played between the ears'
> A reminder that the mental part of the game of golf is critical.

**'A good drive matter-eth not,
if you don't pay attention to the 2nd shot!'**

'Eyes down, ball goes up'
> If you keep your eyes down, the ball will go up... and vice versa!

3. GOLF!

Did you know...?

Golf was banned in Scotland from 1457 to 1502 to ensure citizens wouldn't waste time when preparing for an English invasion.

... and Some Golfing Terms

Scratch golfer: an excellent golfer with a Zero handicap.

GUR: Ground Under Repair—If your ball has landed in one of these areas, retrieve it and drop it no closer to the hole—no penalty.

Drop Area: If your tee shot was unsuccessful and landed in a water hazard or out of bounds on a Par 3 hole, there will usually be a marked Drop Area from which you will take your next shot (3rd stroke).

Relief: Your ball may be moved, without penalty, from interference by an immovable object, abnormal ground conditions, or from the wrong green.

Provisional Ball: another ball played for a ball that may be lost outside a water hazard or out of bounds.

Casual Water: A temporary accumulation of water on the course. You do not have to stand in or hit a ball out of casual water. Drop the ball no closer to the hole—no penalty.

Chili dip: A miss-hit chip shot.

Choke down: To hold the club lower on the grip.

The Dance Floor: a slang term for the green.

Sandbagger: a golfer who inflates his/her handicap to gain an advantage.

These are only a few terms in the world of golf! Heard something you don't understand? Either ask another golfer or look it up on the internet!

Golf Quiz!

Find answers on

1. Which club do you use most in a golf game?

1. *page 7*

2. What is a bogey?

2. *page 58*

3. Why are golf balls numbered?

3. *page 13*

4. How many clubs may a player carry?

4. *page 67*

5. What does a Cue Card do for you?

5. *page 28*

6. What is GUR?

6. *page 82*

7. What is a 'golden ferret'?

7. *page 48*

8. Who is responsible for knowing the Rules of Golf!

8. *page 56 or 67*

3. GOLF!

Did you know...?

A golf ball travels farther at high altitude, and in warm weather.

Couldn't have Done it without...

Many, many thanks to the countless **junior golfers** who I have approached as they hung around golf courses waiting to play. My question to them was... 'What do you think a beginning junior golfer should know about golf?' Answers were remarkably similar—this game is fun, you must be honest, you must be patient, you should practice, lessons are fun and important, golf helps you focus and concentrate, you can make new friends. These responses were very gratifying—our new young golfers are well on their way to enjoying the game, and by association are absorbing many important life skills.

Thanks also go to golf professionals, friends and relatives, who kindly critiqued this material and cheered from the sidelines. They include...

Susan Briske, LPGA Class A, Director of Golf, Peach Tree Country Club, CA

Dale Broughton, CPGA Teaching Professional, Valley Golf Centre, Victoria BC

Patty Curtiss, LPGA Class A, Indian Wells G&CC, CA, and Coach of the Washington State Junior Girls

J.L. Davidson, advice from Texas

Sarah & Eric Francis, Excellent golfers; Eric: Sports Journalist, Calgary AB

Jim Goddard, Head Professional, Cordova Bay Golf Course

Jason Giesbrecht, Director of Golf, Royal Colwood Golf Club, Victoria, BC Canada

Jody Jackson, LPGA Class A, Technical Director of Golf, BCGA Vancouver, BC

Alison Krone & **Dale Jackson**, keen golfers; Dale: Trustee, Pacific Coast Golf Association

Stormin' Norm Jackson, Head Professional Cowichan Golf Club

Gerry Kelly, my soul-mate who is a wonderful sounding board and is seriously addicted to golf

Craig & Sue Kelly, cheerleaders from afar

Kyle Long, Head PGA Professional, Meadow Lake Resort, Montana

Randy & Agnes Pewarchuk, parents of 3 Championship Junior golfers

Margaret Price, Elementary School Principal and keen golfer

Ken Bellemare, who helped with the title, and

The WWW group that I golf with on a weekly basis.

Invaluable in the design and illustration of this book are Miriam MacPhail, a brilliant graphic designer, and Soren Henrich, a very clever illustrator. The technical side includes Erwin Reisler and the staff at Bayside Press.

The Author—Who Am I?

I come from a family of golfers. My husband, Gerry, is an excellent golfer, a student of the game and most often can be located on a golf course. Both our children and their families are golfers. Sarah and Eric golf in Calgary, AB, Craig and Sue golf in Geneva, Switzerland. My Dad loved to golf with his children and grandchildren. At age 86, after parring the 17th hole, he died on the golf course, playing with his best friends, on a beautiful day, doing what he loved.

With a degree in Education and Physical Education, I enjoyed teaching young people. After writing a successful women's golf book, junior golfers inspired me to write **Ready... Set... GOLF!**. The values that one can learn on the golf course will help young people set high standards for themselves and contribute to an enjoyable and successful life.

Young Golfers' Code

- Respect fellow golfers and the golf course.

- Be courteous and polite at all times.

- Play fair, be honest and take responsibility for your actions.

- Improve by listening and concentrating.

- Practise hard and when you play, think before you act.

- Look smart and stay healthy.

- Enjoy the game and your partners.